Remembrance Day and the Poppy

Helen Cox Cannons

raintree

Raintree is an imprint of Capstone Global Library Limited, a company incorporated in England and Wales having its registered office at 264 Banbury Road, Oxford, OX2 7DY – Registered company number: 6695582

www.raintree.co.uk
myorders@raintree.co.uk

Edited by Clare Lewis
Designed by Steve Mead
Picture research by Kelly Garvin
Production by Helen McCreath
Originated by Capstone Global Library
Printed and bound in the United Kingdom

ISBN 978 1 4747 1436 5 (hardback)
19 18 17 16 15
10 9 8 7 6 5 4 3 2 1

ISBN 978 1 4747 1447 1 (paperback)
22 21 20 19 18
10 9 8 7 6 5 4 3 2

British Library Cataloguing in Publication Data
A full catalogue record for this book is available from the British Library.

Acknowledgements
The author and publisher are grateful to the following for permission to reproduce copyright material:
We would like to thank the following for permission to reproduce images: Alamy: amer ghazzal, 12, Andrew Wilson, 7, John Frost Newspapers, 6, Realimage, 14; Corbis: Demptix/Velar Grant, 15; Getty Images: Matt Cardy, 21; Newscom: Ingram Publishing, 13, Mondadori, 19, Reuters/Chris Wattie, 11, REX/Brian Harris, 16, Xinhua News Agency/Sergel Bachlakov, 8, ZUMA Press/Ben Birchall, 9, ZUMA Press/Ben Cawthra, 4, ZUMA Press/Fiona Hanson, 10, ZUMA Press/I-Images, 20; Shutterstock: BasPhoto, 5, EtiAmmos, 18, Everett Historical, cover (war scene), Gonzalo Sanchez, 22, kostrez, cover (poppy)

Every effort has been made to contact copyright holders of material reproduced in this book. Any omissions will be rectified in subsequent printings if notice is given to the publisher.

Contents

Some words are shown in bold, **like this.** You can
find out what they mean by looking in the glossary.

What is Remembrance Day?

Remembrance Day takes place every year in November. On this day, we remember soldiers who died in World War I (1914–18) and other wars.

On Remembrance Day we wear poppies. People in many countries take part in special events. They also lay **wreaths** around **war memorials**.

WORLD WAR I
1914-1918

TO THE
IMPERISHABLE MEMORY
OF OUR
GALLA

WORLD WAR 2
1939-1945

When is Remembrance Day?

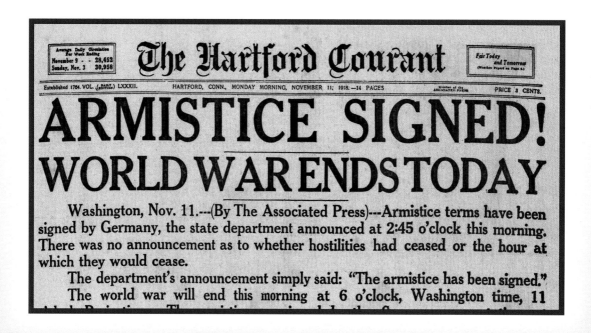

World War I ended on 11th November 1918, with an **armistice**. An armistice was a peace document signed by all the leaders of the warring countries. So, Remembrance Day is held on 11th November every year.

The second Sunday of November is called Remembrance Sunday. There are special church services and **processions**. Cubs and Brownies often take part. Perhaps you have done this, too.

Why do we have a two-minute silence?

The **armistice** that ended World War I took place at 11am on 11th November, 1918. So, this was the 11th hour of the 11th day of the 11th month. At this time each year, we hold a two-minute silence.

People in schools, offices and shops stop what they are doing and stay silent for two minutes. This gives us time to think about all the soldiers who have died in wars around the world.

Who are veterans?

Veterans are people who have served in the **Armed Forces**. There are no veterans of World War I still living today.

There are many veterans worldwide who fought in World War II (1939–45). On Remembrance Day, veterans wear their uniforms. They also wear any medals that they were given for their bravery.

Where is Remembrance Day held?

Many countries around the world hold Remembrance Day. In Australia and New Zealand, people also have Anzac Day. It especially celebrates Australian and New Zealand soldiers who died in wars.

Around 100,000 Canadian soldiers died fighting in World Wars I and II. In Canada, Remembrance Day is a public holiday in most regions.

Why is Remembrance Day sometimes called Poppy Day?

Sometimes people call Remembrance Day Poppy Day. Across the world, people wear poppies to show support for soldiers. Poppies have become a **symbol** of hope and remembrance.

In the UK, poppies are sold by members of the Royal British Legion. The Royal British Legion is a charity that helps **veterans** and families of soldiers who died in battle. It was formed in 1921.

Why poppies?

Poppies grow in the fields in France where the battles during World War I took place. They stopped growing during wartime but flowered again afterwards.

"In Flanders fields the poppies blow
Between the crosses, row on row,
That mark our place; and in the sky
The larks, still bravely singing, fly
Scarce heard amid the guns below...

...We shall not sleep,
though poppies grow
In Flanders fields."

John McCrae was a Canadian doctor. He fought in World War I. He wrote a poem called "In Flanders Fields" about the poppies in France.

Who was "The Poppy Lady"?

An American lady, Moina Michael, loved John McCrae's poem. In 1918, she decided to make red, silk poppies. Then she went to huge efforts to make the poppy the official symbol of remembrance.

Moina Michael became known as "The Poppy Lady". When the British Legion formed in 1921, they ordered 9 million poppies for the UK. By 11th November that year, the poppies had all sold out.

Remembrance Day and the Royal family

The Royal family plays an important part in Remembrance Day events. The Queen lays a **wreath** at the Cenotaph. The Cenotaph is a famous **war memorial** in London.

Members of the Royal family also
visit countries around the world for
Remembrance Day. Prince Harry went to
Afghanistan on Remembrance Day in 2014.

100 years of remembrance

In 2014, it was 100 years since World War I began. To mark this, 888,246 **ceramic** poppies were laid out in the Tower of London moat. Each poppy was for the death of a British World War I soldier.

Glossary

armed forces all the military groups of a country. The air force, army and navy are all armed forces.

armistice agreement between people or countries to stop war

ceramic made of baked clay

procession people walking or travelling in an ordered way

symbol something that stands for something else

veteran someone who has served in the armed forces

war memorial special statue or place where soldiers who have died are remembered

wreath ring of flowers. Wreaths are often laid on graves or memorials.

Find out more

Remembrance Day (Popcorn History), Kay Barnham (Wayland, 2010)

Remembrance Day (Start-up History), Jane Bingham (Franklin Watts, 2014)

Remembrance Day (Great Events), Gillian Clements (Franklin Watts, 2014)

Index